Also available:

YOGA FOR CATS

TRAUDL AND WALTER REINER

with Simone Stein

ASTROLOGY FOR

CATS

Translated by Anthea Bell

LONDON
VICTOR GOLLANCZ LTD
1992

First published in Great Britain August 1992
by Victor Gollancz Ltd
14 Henrietta Street, London WC2E 8QJ

A catalogue record for this book
is available from the British Library

0 575 05348 8

Printed in Great Britain by
Cambus Litho Ltd

Which is the right cat for your family? You should consider the question carefully, for many a velvet paw conceals sharp claws. And why does your cat behave as it does, and not some other way? This book of feline horoscopes reveals all . . .

Contents

CHARACTER:
Impulsive, impatient, aggressive

ELEMENT:
Fire

COMPATIBLE STAR SIGNS:
Sagittarius, Leo, Aquarius

Aries

21 MARCH – 20 APRIL

Character

The Aries cat likes the limelight and always manages to hold centre stage. In fact, you could say it's a bit of a show-off. It loves admiration, is full of self-confidence and once it's got an idea in its head won't let go in a hurry. This means that Aries cats are very good at learning tricks and they work hard at polishing up their acts. Even closed doors are no problem for these clever cats.

All this activity makes it ravenous, so don't be surprised if your pet's taste in food runs to quantity rather than quality. But, though the Aries cat may not be particularly choosy, it does insist that everything it eats is absolutely fresh. If not, it will show its displeasure by some angry tail-lashing followed by the sulks, and then it will probably go next door to see if something better is on offer.

Lifestyle

The Aries cat is one of life's go-getters; it grabs anything it can lay its paws on and puts great mental and physical effort into the attempt, but it just can't bear to wait. It knows exactly what it wants, and wants it now! Its recklessness often lands it in trouble and it shows no consideration for either your valuable china col-

lection or its own safety in pursuit of its aims. Beware! It's probably wise to put away anything that might suffer from your furry friend's enthusiasm – or take out an 'all risks' policy.

Never forget: your cat owns your home – and your garden. The stormy-natured Aries cat likes the great outdoors, where it has the space to indulge in some real feline self-expression.

Personal relationships

If you want to keep an excitable Aries cat under control you have to show it who's in charge. At heart it respects a strong, firm character and will take merciless advantage of any weakness you display. It likes playing with children but will expect *them* to go along with *its* whims and fancies.

The Aries cat is boisterous with other cats and often comes home from its nocturnal outings rather the worse for wear – hungry, dirty and scarred. It isn't afraid of larger animals either. It will defend its own territory fiercely against a large, ferocious dog – but then might confuse the poor creature by falling madly in love with it. Speaking of love, Aries cats are definitely the conquering type. When an Aries cat sets its sights on a likely mate, it usually gets its way. Once it has begun a relationship, however, it can be soppily romantic.

The Aries cat tends to show cupboard love for humans. If it rubs affectionately against your legs, it is probably saying it's hungry or thirsty. And, if it volunteers to do a trick for you, it will expect to be rewarded with an extra helping of goodies to fortify it for a night on the tiles.

CHARACTER:
Persevering, patient, realistic

ELEMENT:
Earth

COMPATIBLE STAR SIGNS:
Virgo, Cancer, Capricorn

Taurus

21 APRIL – 20 MAY

Character

Taurean cats are unlike most others: they're not playful, capricious or particularly athletic; nor are they deceitful or open to bribery. The Taurean cat appears to be very laid-back; it exudes an air of nobility whatever its station in life. Even the ordinary farmyard cat has a look of distinction about it.

A Taurean cat goes to no trouble and causes none. Anything for a quiet life! It values its own possessions and doesn't like sharing its dish, its basket or its toys. However, it also respects other people's property. It will eat from another cat's dish or sleep on a strange blanket only in the direst emergency. It hates going away and regards car journeys as sheer torture – but if you put it in a cattery it feels betrayed.

As for diet, punctuality is more important than variety. It will happily eat the same flavour of cat food for days on end, as long as you serve it on the dot!

Lifestyle

The patient, persevering Taurean cat isn't easily upset. But, if its need for peace and stability seems really threatened, watch out! Your usually laid-back kitty can throw terrible, destructive tantrums and nothing will calm it down. Usually the best plan is to leave the furious little monster alone until the storm has blown over.

The Taurean cat loves dozing and day-dreaming and, even when fully awake, hates to be disturbed. It will sit for hours musing on the meaning of life, or the age-old problem of the totally unnecessary existence of dogs in the world, so be careful not to interrupt its train of thought.

Personal relationships

Taurean cats are faithful to their owners. Once a Taurean cat has taken you to its heart it will do anything for you. It will keep on loving you even if you go away for a long time. It enjoys looking after children but has a tendency to get too involved. So, if your offspring goes missing, try looking in the cat's basket.

The Taurean cat is happiest in a small, harmonious family where no one expects too much of it. Pay it the respect it feels it deserves and it will be in its element.

Maximum comfort for minimum effort: such is the ambition of the Taurean cat, so it's quite likely to be constant for life in affairs of the heart. Once a Taurean cat has found the right mate, it becomes completely devoted. Taurean cats do best with placid companions who don't inject too much excitement into the daily feline round.

CHARACTER:
Inquisitive, sociable, unpredictable

☆

ELEMENT:
Air

☆

COMPATIBLE STAR SIGNS:
Aquarius, Libra

Gemini

21 MAY – 21 JUNE

Character

One moment cheerful, playful, inquisitive – the next, withdrawn, hissing, inaccessible: that's the typical Gemini cat. It's everything a cat is popularly supposed to be, and more. Streetwise and very aware of what's going on, it always puts itself first.

There isn't much a Gemini cat won't try and it invariably makes interesting discoveries. It can learn, for instance, how to open a door with a little determined paw-work – or how to smash a boiled egg by tipping it off the table. These ingenious tricks are designed to amuse and surprise you and it will react most violently if you scold it. In fact, show it you're cross and you'll be sorry! It will be even more contrary than usual, winding itself around your legs to trip you up or settling down on your new black jacket. Once it realises you are seriously angry, however, it will turn on the charm. The sociable Gemini cat purrs more and louder than almost any other cat.

Lifestyle

Owners of Gemini cats know that satisfying their gourmet tastes is not easy. A Gemini cat likes plenty of variety and naturally its cat food must be the very best available. It may greedily devour a helping of tuna today, only to turn it down with contempt tomorrow. If you ignore its finicky tastes, it will pick what it fancies out of its dish and leave the rest.

Sleep is not important to a Gemini cat. Life is too short to be dozed away! So it only takes cat-naps. It doesn't mind being woken up for an amusing game – but your idea of amusement had better be good.

Personal relationships

The Gemini cat needs close contact with as many people as possible. It's an expert at making advances. It will rub lovingly around the legs of a total stranger, allow a passing acquaintance to stroke it, or jump on a visitor's lap; but though it may flatter people it knows the difference between friend and foe. If your Gemini cat avoids someone, you can be sure that person doesn't like animals.

People who really lose their hearts to their pets would do better to get a faithful Taurean cat. There's always a risk that your Gemini cat will simply walk out of your life. Despite its sociability with humans, it's not a very good companion for other cats as it soon gets bored with feline company.

When a Gemini cat falls in love, however, it throws its usual values overboard and adopts the habits of its beloved – for a while, anyway. The fire of love never burns long in the fickle Gemini heart, but it burns fiercely, leaving no trace behind.

CHARACTER:
Sensitive, tidy, emotional

ELEMENT:
Water

COMPATIBLE STAR SIGNS:
Pisces, Scorpio, Taurus

Cancer

22 JUNE – 22 JULY

Character

The Cancerian cat has all the airs and graces of a prima donna, along with the sensitivity of a seismograph. It wants to be cherished and admired. It believes the whole world revolves around it and the least little thing can upset it. It plays on its delicate constitution to get extra attention. In fact, if you don't spoil it rotten, it may even develop psychosomatic illnesses. Cancer is a water sign, and your cat's emotional life reflects the ebb and flow of the tides. But, when it feels like it, it can sit placidly for hours like a Buddha.

The Cancerian cat is a brilliant actor. If it thinks a game has gone on for too long, it pretends to be exhausted, but once something new attracts its attention it instantly perks up, coming to see what's on offer.

The Cancerian cat is genuinely scared of thunderstorms and will hide in a corner or, trembling, seek safety in your arms, long before the thunder and lightning actually start.

Lifestyle

The Cancerian cat always seems rather weary and disinclined for physical exertion and gets what it wants by appealing to your kindness and sympathy. It will pretend it's got no appetite and is only eating to please you. This fussy cat has its own special preferences and sometimes won't eat just because it doesn't like the colour of a new dish. It chooses its bed for neatness and warmth and will always prefer your lap or a nice pile of freshly ironed shirts to a basket. Its tidy nature means that it returns to the same sleeping place regularly. The Cancerian cat is a good companion. It's not destructive and treasures your ornaments almost as much as you do.

Personal relationships

Even the quiet, unobtrusive Cancerian cat won't stay in the background for ever, and it likes to live with a strong human. Deep in its heart it wants its family to make life easy for it. It may be a little while before it feels sure of you and becomes really loving. If an adult Cancerian cat is taken into a new home, it may be stand-offish for weeks or even months. However, once it has decided you're worthy of its love, it will be touchingly devoted and try to keep its whims and fancies under control.

Its relationships with other cats are complicated, since its feelings are easily hurt and it displays them with alacrity. Living with other cats is hard enough but it's almost impossible to keep a Cancerian cat with a dog, unless the dog is ready to accept it as boss.

The Cancerian cat is a lyrical and romantic lover, but some Cancerian cats never fall in love because their ideals are too high and they won't compromise.

CHARACTER:
Independent, bold, optimistic, trusting

ELEMENT:
Fire

☆

COMPATIBLE STAR SIGNS:
Aries, Sagittarius, Capricorn

Leo

23 JULY – 23 AUGUST

Character

To be born under Leo, the 'royal sign', as astrologers used to call it, is lucky, even for a cat. The Leo cat, individual and independent, pads its way through life with head held high, despising lesser mortals. It is only too aware of its aristocratic position and would never stoop to performing silly, attention-seeking tricks – for it knows, of course, that it is always the centre of interest.

Leos are rarely inclined to lie quietly doing nothing. They love the thrill of the chase but even town cats are realistic enough not to waste their time on hopeless pursuit. Let common-or-garden cats wear themselves out to no good purpose. The regal Leo cat knows what it's doing – although you may find it sitting by the plughole in the bath for hours on end, waiting for a mouse to come out!

Lifestyle

The Leo cat is in no doubt that it is King of the Beasts. It spends hours grooming itself until its fur is silky and shining. No sooner are you out of the room than the Leo cat is admiring itself in the mirror. It loves having its photo taken and relishes compliments. Indeed, its vanity knows no bounds. Appearances are soon forgotten though, if an adventure is in prospect; then it doesn't shrink from a bit of dirt – or a fight.

As to diet: it has an insatiable appetite for fresh meat, and adores liver, but if you keep your royal cat waiting too long for its food, you'll have to make up for it by offering an extra titbit and plenty of stroking, or it will punish you by showing some lordly bad temper.

Personal relationships

Never, *never* condescend to a Leo cat. Your pet wants to be your equal and will never forgive being patronised. Worst of all, it hates indifference: a Leo cat would rather be shouted at than ignored.

If a Leo cat feels loved and appreciated, it will do anything for its humans. It is trusting and friendly and not afraid of strangers. But it will bravely square up to anything it sees as a threat to you, so be careful not to pet any strange cats, avoid romping with children and, above all, keep a proper distance from dogs. Many a harmless canine has been scarred for life by a jealous, aggressive Leo cat.

The Leo cat has many feline friends who respect its strength and don't mind being bossed about. It doesn't play, it holds court and, as not all cats are prepared to knuckle under, it has its fair share of enemies ready to steal its glory or even the food off its plate.

If your Leo cat ever goes missing, don't worry – it's probably out looking for more atten-tion. In a relationship it needs the lion's share of adoration, so the successful mate will be the one that best flatters its vanity.

♍

CHARACTER:
Prudent, sensible, critical

ELEMENT:
Earth

COMPATIBLE STAR SIGNS:
Capricorn, Taurus, Pisces

Virgo

24 AUGUST – 23 SEPTEMBER

Character

The Virgo cat is critical, pernickety and a bit of a perfectionist. It is stronger on logic and intelligence than natural instinct. It's also an acute observer, with a calculating nature: it knows that the knitting you are holding will prevent you from stroking it, and it won't even try to jump on your lap. It will simply bite through your wool instead. It soon learns where you keep good things to eat and employs almost human cunning to help itself when no one is watching. A sealed milk carton? Easy! A film-wrapped piece of cheese? Kitten's play! Of course, it knows quite well that these delicacies are not meant for cats, but a Virgo cat has no conscience. Scold it and it acts deaf. It will be magnanimous enough to ignore your anger, just so long as it got what it was after.

The only thing that will stop a Virgo cat from pursuing its own ends is danger, which it can spot a mile off. Safety first is its motto. If it does happen to climb a tree or do acrobatics on the furniture, it makes sure it's not likely to fall.

Born under the earth sign, the Virgo cat loves plants, including your lovingly tended house plants, and you had better let it have them. A Virgo cat lives on its own terms. Try and impose your views on it and it will retreat into silence and nothing you can do will draw it out.

Lifestyle

Never let the Virgo cat out of your sight for long. It will use any chance it gets to steal a march on you. A table laid for a meal is a temptation it simply can't resist. It likes to eat the same food as you – even pickles if you happen to fancy them.

A Virgo cat likes everything to be neat and clean. Leave a comb, a glove or a lipstick carelessly lying about and your Virgo cat will tidy them up so efficiently that you'll never find them again. You must keep its litter tray as clean as an operating theatre, or it will look for what it considers a more suitable spot – and if you don't agree, well, it was your fault!

Personal relationships

On first acquaintance, your Virgo cat will regard you with a critical eye. It will sit for ages pretending indifference but all the time it will be observing you closely and drawing its own conclusions. If it decides further intimacy with you is worthwhile, it becomes a most affectionate house cat, charming and anxious to please.

The Virgo cat gets on quite well with other cats – at a distance. If obliged to share its home with other pets it is easily upset because of its tidy nature, and that's no joke for the newcomer, who must either adjust to the Virgo cat or stick to its own territory – preferably at the far end of the house.

In affairs of the heart, the Virgo cat moves slowly and deliberately, first observing from a distance, then taking a sniff, then perhaps … but all in good time. The Virgo cat doesn't give way to instinct until it is really in the mood.

CHARACTER:
Luxury-loving, good-humoured, irresolute

☆

ELEMENT:
Air

☆

COMPATIBLE STAR SIGNS:
Aquarius, Gemini

Libra

24 SEPTEMBER – 23 OCTOBER

Character

The Libran cat thinks it has star quality and it demands a lot. A high standard of living and elegant surroundings are vitally important. As it has loads of charm, and usually looks entrancing, it gets its own way quite easily but, even when things go wrong, it seldom loses its temper. It merely turns its attention to some new desirable object it would like to acquire.

The Libran cat loves to be surrounded by admirers, whether feline or human, just so long as they are fans. Despite its airs and graces, it tends to win all hearts. Everyone likes a Libran cat.

Its poise vanishes the moment it falls in love. Then it forgets all about good behaviour. As the female Libran cat has difficulty making up her mind, there are often fierce fights between her suitors. She keeps a safe distance from the actual battlefield, but her vain little soul rather enjoys it – not that she bestows her favours on the happy victor right away. Far from it! She gives him the once-over first. She's far too discriminating to go off with any old tom cat, even if he has won her fairly.

Lifestyle

The Libran cat hates conflict, loves domestic harmony and to this end will always do its best to behave well and build up a good relationship with you. It takes great care of itself and its surroundings, is affectionate and loving and will even come when you call.

A favourite pastime of the Libran cat is watching humans at work. It can sit glued to the spot for hours, observing your every move, trying to make sense of what you're doing. Even as an adult cat, it is always playful. If you don't give a Libran cat toys of its own, it will seek out a bunch of dried flowers or the contents of your workbasket to play with. When it comes to food, the Libran cat is not difficult or especially fussy to feed, and has no objection to eating left-overs.

Personal relationships

The Libran cat conducts its personal relationships on the 'cat and mouse' principle: wildly affectionate to humans and other cats one day, stand-offish the next. This is only meant as harmless flirting. At the bottom of its capricious heart, the Libran cat is always affectionate and peace-loving. That, and its playfulness, makes it an ideal pet for children and it is usually particularly fond of them.

You'll quite often see a Libran cat following its favourite human like a dog. It loves sleeping on a nice soft bed and however often you shoo it away, it will be back next moment, whether you're in bed or not. It may even pretend to be ill, believing you couldn't be hard-hearted enough to turn it off then. Think yourself lucky if you can at least train it to prefer the end of the bed and not take up the whole pillow.

♏

CHARACTER:
Patient, jealous, obstinate

ELEMENT:
Water

COMPATIBLE STAR SIGNS:
Cancer, Pisces

Scorpio

24 OCTOBER – 22 NOVEMBER

Character

Cats born under Mars can be really tough characters, and it's no good trying to fob them off with anything second rate. Only the best will do for the Scorpio cat.

The Scorpio cat likes to investigate its surroundings and is constantly exploring every nook and cranny of your home. With its inventive mind, it can think up all sorts of new uses for household furnishings and other items. Many a Scorpio cat has turned a pair of velvet curtains into a climbing frame, or settled down for a siesta in the drum of the washing machine.

A Scorpio cat needs to be in charge. If you're prepared to go along with that, are happy to welcome its friends into your home, and provide plenty of entertainment, it can be absolutely charming.

The Scorpio cat is patient and too proud to accept help. Scold it and it sulks. It wants its share of everything — from the ham in your sandwich to your newly uphol- stered armchair. Whatever you may think, your Scorpio cat knows you are really its slave and, if you haven't noticed — well, that's a tribute to your cat's in- telligence.

Lifestyle

Your Scorpio cat hates being cooped up indoors while you're out shopping or at work. However, it can always console itself in your absence with a good TV programme.

Scorpio cats are happiest living on a farm where they can roam freely and have adventures. They are good hunters and can survive for days in the open country without human help. They will often stand up to other animals and will even take on a fully grown sheepdog.

In fact, your Scorpio cat lives life to the full. It will eat anything – and sometimes has to bring it up again – but whatever it does is done with natural dignity. Even an ordinary moggy Scorpio has something special about it.

Personal relationships

You can't ignore the love of a Scorpio cat. Once it has taken you to its heart, it is very possessive, wanting your attention at all times. It gets jealous very easily and is seldom content with casual affection – it wants everything. It likes to play rough games with its claws out but then turns really loving. So expect your pet to lead a chaotic love life: scratched faces, missing tufts of fur and torn ears are all signs of the amorous Scorpio cat. Even so, it usually captivates its chosen mate just as it captivated you.

Other cats regard the Scorpio cat as quarrelsome and dominating. A bit of an aggressive egotist, it likes to prove itself the better cat in a fight; of course it does – it's programmed to be a champ. Best of all, it will win the hearts of all your family and friends and you'll prob- ably find that when people are making their wills your cat may well be left a legacy.

CHARACTER:
Optimistic, arrogant, roving

ELEMENT:
Fire

COMPATIBLE STAR SIGNS:
Aries, Leo

Sagittarius

23 NOVEMBER – 21 DECEMBER

Character

The adventurous Sagittarian cat is a free spirit and a real high flyer – which means it may also come a cropper.

Always optimistic, it never learns from its mistakes and will nonchalantly write off a failure one moment, only to embark on some new and reckless adventure the next. In fact, nothing will shake its belief in itself and its own capabilities.

The Sagittarian cat is definitely the outdoors type and can't bear to be confined in small spaces. It isn't easy to keep this liberty-loving cat happy in a small flat in town. Shut indoors all the time, it tends to use its excess energy in mischief and doing expensive damage. You may find it trying out its claws on your curtains, upsetting flower vases and having boxing matches with your house plants as it tries to work off its frustration.

Lifestyle

Considering the strenuous life a Sagittarian cat leads, it isn't surprising that it's always hungry, but it likes quality as well as quantity. It needs good protein-rich food and can consume amazing quantities. As it converts most of the calories into energy, it doesn't usually grow fat.

The Sagittarian cat is fussy about its bed, which should be in a quiet but easily accessible spot. It likes to be near its humans, but able to go out prowling at night. With its adaptable and restless nature, the Sagittarian cat enjoys going on holiday with you. It prefers four-star hotels, but will make do with something more modest: the opportunity to go out exploring is what really matters. Adventurous cats like these run risks, so it might be wise to put wire netting over windows high above the ground, and it wouldn't do any harm to take out pet insurance.

Personal relationships

The Sagittarian cat will get on with anyone who doesn't try to cramp its style. Children love its playfulness and lack of real aggression. Sagittarian cats are passionately fond of birds. If you want to be on really good terms with your pet, buy it a budgie – in a cat-proof cage (just in case its natural instincts get the better of it).

It is generally friendly but a little aloof with other cats. The quiet, happy understanding that can evolve between the Sagittarian cat and its pet budgie seldom develops with one of its own kind. When your pet does fall for a conquering tom or a beautiful female, however, it will probably bring the object of its affections home, and you had better not disapprove! But, alas, its love affairs soon burn out.

A Sagittarian cat does its utmost to ensure the survival of the species. Sagittarian toms father countless kittens and the love life of the female is one long adventure, crammed with assignations, partings and unplanned families. There's nothing you can do about this, so it's best to ignore it.

♑

CHARACTER:
Headstrong, clever, melancholy

ELEMENT:
Earth

COMPATIBLE STAR SIGNS:
Taurus, Virgo, Leo

Capricorn

22 DECEMBER – 20 JANUARY

Character

You could almost call a Capricorn cat foxy: it's cunning, withdrawn and extremely clever. A Capricorn cat believes nothing it hasn't seen for itself. Capricorn cats are ambitious. Once they start something they don't give up easily – whether it's fishing a hairpin out of a crack in the floorboards or making friends with the dog next door. Nothing, not even the most tempting delicacies will divert them from their purpose.

The Capricorn cat is always quick to spot any danger and will take steps to avoid it, so it runs little risk of getting hurt.

Although generally well-balanced, the Capricorn cat needs a lot of human and animal contact and is likely to get depressed and melancholy without it. It's rather self-important and likes a feeling of power, but as long as it feels appreciated by you, it will be a happy and affectionate pet.

Lifestyle

The Capricorn cat is a moderate eater with a good metabolism. It prefers high-quality food but doesn't demand anything too exotic. Regular helpings of what it likes are all it needs to satisfy it. Make sure its dish is clean, for Capricorn cats have good table manners. As they're not especially active, any excess food turns to fat.

Rest is more important than food to the Capricorn cat, and it needs plenty of time to meditate. Despite its need for contact, it is inclined to be reclusive and will indulge this tendency frequently – occupying your desk-top for hours on end in pursuit of the quiet life. You'll have to adjust your working hours to suit your cat, not the other way round.

It hates change, so before rearranging your furniture, you should prepare your cat in advance. Give it an inch and it will take a mile so be careful about letting it get into bed with you – it will expect to sleep there every night!

Personal relationships

Although your Capricorn cat may be rather reserved in some ways, it makes a good and loving companion. It's not happy being on the bottom rung of the family ladder though, and will do anything to rise up the social scale. It always feels superior to a new baby and will either mother the infant or watch it jealously to see if it's getting too much attention. Acquiring another, younger cat for it to boss around will make it feel better.

Capricorn cats are rather awkward lovers. They don't like making the first move, are slow to become enamoured, and when they do bring the chosen cat home, will watch suspiciously to see if you treat it properly. Passionate love is foreign to the Capricorn cat's nature – in this respect it is the coolest of all the star signs.

CHARACTER:
Independent, temperamental, inventive

ELEMENT:
Air

COMPATIBLE STAR SIGNS:
Libra, Gemini, Aries

Aquarius

21 JANUARY – 19 FEBRUARY

Character

An Aquarian cat is a complicated creature, often at odds with itself. Part of it wants to be loving and affectionate, another part feels duty bound to show its claws. It begs for milk and then sits irresolutely in front of its bowl. This unpredictable behaviour is guaranteed to worry its owner – and it does enjoy keeping you on your toes. What fun it is to be such a difficult, provocative cat – always the centre of attention!

It is a most enterprising cat, able to brush off its failures with ease: an Aquarian cat planning to achieve greatness won't let small things deter it, and a gap in the fence where it once got stuck, is still endlessly fascinating.

Its ingenuity gets it into the most unlikely places – usually places you'd rather it didn't go – and it will happily stay hidden away for hours. So make sure you check cupboards and the inside of the tumbler dryer before closing the doors.

The Aquarian cat has a limitless need for love and if scolded will act insulted and go away to hide, but arouse its curiosity or its appetite and it will come out, playful as ever, as if nothing had happened.

Lifestyle

On its own, the Aquarian cat is a quiet well-balanced animal that seldom gets silly ideas. But once it's got an audience, it indulges in the most wilful, temperamental, attention-seeking behaviour. It is changeable about food. Today's favourite flavour may be turned down flat tomorrow. What it gets is often less important than how it gets it. If you go to the trouble of holding the bowl and enticing it with loving words, its appetite will return in no time.

In spite of its contrary behaviour towards you, the Aquarian cat has great admiration for everything human. You may not have noticed but it is doing its best to be just like you. So, if you want to know more about yourself, watch your cat!

Personal relationships

An Aquarian cat needs an owner with strong nerves, who loves animals but will not be bossed about. You can't take it to visit friends, or even on holiday, because the mere sight of strangers will alarm it and it will act in a way calculated to put off even the most confirmed animal lover. Nor will it welcome visitors to your home and it will hiss and spit at them until they've gone. Then, of course, it lays on the charm thickly to win back your hearts. Needless to say, it always succeeds!

With children it can easily become a tyrant; it's not happy unless everyone is dancing to its tune. The one thing you *can't* do is have no relationship at all with an Aquarian cat.

'The cat next door' is not the right mate for your pet. It does not like anything ordinary. 'All cats may be grey in the dark', as the old proverb goes, but your Aquarian cat wouldn't agree. It falls in love with exotic cats, or cats who can teach it clever tricks … who knows what surprises your Aquarian cat may yet have in store for you?

CHARACTER:
Sensitive, dreamy, instinctive

☆

ELEMENT:
Water

☆

COMPATIBLE STAR SIGNS:
Cancer, Scorpio, Virgo

Pisces

20 FEBRUARY – 20 MARCH

Character

Even as a kitten, a Pisces cat shows its unscrupulous nature. You will never get it to do anything by means of sweet reason, let alone force. A Pisces cat makes its own rules and lives by them. Once it's decided to spend the day out of doors, nothing and no one can lure it back in. If it thinks it is time for a nap, it will pick a dustbin or mixing bowl of its choice and settle down, never mind what you say.

Sometimes it will start dozing in the middle of a game: all of a sudden it loses interest in the ball of wool it was eagerly chasing a moment ago, falls asleep and starts dreaming – very vividly, judging by the way it twitches in its sleep. The Pisces cat is of a gentle disposition and won't get angry if you disturb it when it's sleeping. It learns from its mistakes, however, and will make sure it is better hidden the next time it wants to indulge in some dreaming.

Lifestyle

Since it has difficulty following anyone else's rules, a Pisces cat fits best into a relaxed household where everyone does their own thing. With natural sensitivity, it quickly learns to distinguish between something which is in its own interests and something that simply makes life easier for you. Naturally, it favours the former, but if you have convinced it of your absolute devotion it will be touchingly anxious to please you and will be the ideal pet.

With unerring instinct, the Pisces cat picks up human moods and reacts to them. If you need comforting, it will rub gently round your legs. If you want entertaining, it will lay on a show. However, it can go too far in forcing its kind attention on you and may carry on long after you've had enough of watching its furry antics.

Personal relationships

In its love affairs, the sensitive Pisces cat is disastrously inclined to put its faith in magic and other unorthodox methods: it might try telepathy or hypnosis in an attempt to influence its beloved. Unfortunately, as Pisces cats are shy, they are liable to lose their loved ones to less inhibited rivals.

If your cat comes to you as a kitten, it will regard you as a mother substitute and will let you spoil it, ask you to comfort it and generally treat you as its playmate. It has a tendency to become fixated on its human partner and will be jealous of any other relationships you might form – animal or human. If anyone trespasses on its rights, even a dreamy cat like the Pisces will stop at nothing. But, once secure in the knowledge that it is loved and cherished, it will happily share its most personal pleasures with you. That dead mouse or bird it drags in from the garden is meant as a present, so you had better appear delighted or you'll be spurning your pet's affection. God may forgive you; a Pisces cat never will!

The bestselling yoga course for cats!

Whatever its birth sign, your cat will enjoy YOGA FOR CATS, the first feline fitness programme.

Available from Victor Gollancz Ltd

ISBN 0 575 05122 1
£4.99 net